WEIRD UNUSUAL BEHAVIOR AND LIFESTYLE OF ANIMALS

Animals Culture Facts

Dylan Austin

BOWERBIRDS

Fact 1: Imagine being a bird with a passion for interior design. That's the life of a bowerbird! These avian architects build elaborate structures called bowers to attract mates.

Fact 2: But these aren't your average nests. Bowerbirds go all out, using sticks, leaves, flowers, and even bits of plastic and glass to create intricate displays.

Fact 3: What's truly bizarre is that each species has its own unique decorating style. Some prefer a minimalist look, while others go for bold and flashy designs.

Fact 4: But it's not just about looks; it's also about location. Bowerbirds carefully select the site for their bowers, often choosing spots with good visibility to attract more attention.

Fact 5: Once the bower is built, it's time for the real show to begin. Male bowerbirds use their bowers as stages for elaborate courtship displays, showing off their decorating skills to potential mates.

Fact 6: Some species even incorporate optical illusions into their bowers, arranging objects in such a way that they appear larger or smaller than they actually are. It's like avian sleight of hand!

Fact 7: But the competition is fierce in the world of bowerbird romance. Males will often resort to sabotage, destroying rivals' bowers or stealing decorations to enhance their own.

Fact 8: And it's not just the males who are picky; female bowerbirds have high standards too. They'll inspect multiple bowers before choosing a mate, carefully evaluating each one for style and craftsmanship.

Fact 9: But the weirdest part? Once the female has made her choice and mated with the male, she's on her own. Bowerbirds are one of the few bird species that don't form long-term pair bonds.

Fact 10: Despite the elaborate courtship rituals, bowerbirds are actually quite shy and elusive. They prefer to stay hidden in the forest, only venturing out to perform their displays during mating season.

Fact 11: But don't let their demure demeanor fool you; bowerbirds are fiercely territorial. Males will defend their bowers from intruders, engaging in loud squabbles and even physical fights to protect their turf.

Fact 12: And it's not just other birds they have to worry about; bowerbirds are also targeted by predators like snakes and birds of prey. That's why they're always on high alert, ready to flee at the first sign of danger.

Fact 13: Despite their flashy displays, bowerbirds are actually quite picky eaters. They have a specialized diet that includes fruits, insects, and occasionally small lizards or frogs.

Fact 14: But perhaps the most bizarre behavior of all is the Vogelkop bowerbird's love of dancing. Males will perform intricate dance moves, including leaps, twirls, and even moonwalking, to impress potential mates.

Fact 15: Bowerbirds are also known for their vocal talents. Males will sing elaborate songs to serenade females, using a combination of whistles, trills, and chirps to woo their intended partners.

Fact 16: But it's not just about attracting mates; bowerbirds also use their bowers to communicate with each other. They'll leave messages for rivals or potential mates by rearranging objects or adding new decorations to their displays.

Fact 17: And it's not just about looks; bowerbirds also pay attention to scent. Males will often decorate their bowers with aromatic plants or flowers to attract females with their enticing fragrance.

Fact 18: Despite their extravagant displays, bowerbirds are actually quite solitary creatures. They prefer to live alone or in small family groups, only coming together during mating season.

Fact 19: But even in the world of bowerbirds, love isn't always easy. Males will sometimes resort to trickery or deception to attract mates, using fake decorations or even mimicking the calls of other species to lure females to their bowers.

Fact 20: In the end, though, it's all worth it for the chance to pass on their genes to the next generation. Bowerbirds may have weird and unusual behaviors, but it's all in the name of love and reproduction.

DEEP-SEA DWELLERS

Fact 1: Imagine living in a world where sunlight never reaches, the pressure could crush a submarine, and you rely on glowing lights to communicate. That's the reality for deep-sea dwellers like the anglerfish and the gulper eel.

Fact 2: These creatures have evolved some seriously weird adaptations to survive in the abyss. Take the anglerfish, for example. It dangles a bioluminescent lure from its head to attract unsuspecting prey in the darkness.

Fact 3: Meanwhile, the gulper eel has a mouth that can expand to enormous proportions, allowing it to swallow prey much larger than itself. It's like having a built-in vacuum cleaner for the ocean floor!

Fact 4: But perhaps the strangest adaptation of all is the barreleye fish, which has transparent head-casing eyes that can rotate inside its head. It looks like something out of a sci-fi movie!

Fact 5: Living in such extreme conditions requires some serious survival skills. These deep-sea dwellers have developed specialized organs to detect even the tiniest movements and changes in pressure, helping them navigate and hunt in the darkness.

Fact 6: Despite the challenges, the deep sea is teeming with life, from bizarre-looking fish to otherworldly creatures like the vampire squid. It's a reminder that even in the most hostile environments, life finds a way to thrive.

Fact 7: Bioluminescence isn't just for attracting prey; it's also used for communication. Some deep-sea creatures use flashes of light to signal to potential mates or to confuse predators.

Fact 8: Speaking of predators, the deep sea is home to some of the most fearsome hunters on the planet. From giant squid with razor-sharp beaks to ferocious-looking sharks like the goblin shark, it's a literal feeding frenzy down there.

Fact 9: Despite its name, the deep sea isn't actually uniform in temperature. In fact, there are hot vents on the ocean floor that spew out superheated water, creating oases of life in an otherwise barren landscape.

Fact 10: Exploring the deep sea is like exploring an alien world right here on Earth. With every expedition, scientists discover new species and uncover more mysteries about this dark and mysterious realm.

Fact 11: The anglerfish isn't just one species; there are actually over 200 different species, each with its own unique adaptations and hunting strategies.

Fact 12: One of the strangest deep-sea creatures is the vampire squid, which has red eyes and a cloak-like webbing that it can wrap around itself like a cape.

Fact 13: Despite its fearsome appearance, the gulper eel is actually a gentle giant. It feeds primarily on small fish and crustaceans, using its expandable mouth to gulp them down whole.

Fact 14: The barreleye fish isn't the only creature with transparent head-casing eyes; there are also species of deep-sea shrimp and jellyfish that have similar adaptations.

Fact 15: The deep sea is home to some of the oldest and most mysterious creatures on the planet, including the elusive giant squid, which can grow up to 43 feet in length.

Fact 16: Many deep-sea creatures have evolved to be bioluminescent, producing their own light through a chemical reaction in their bodies. This helps them attract prey, communicate with each other, and even deter predators.

Fact 17: Some deep-sea creatures have developed specialized organs called photophores, which contain bioluminescent bacteria or chemicals that produce light. These organs can be found all over their bodies, from their eyes to their fins.

Fact 18: The deep sea is one of the least explored and understood ecosystems on Earth. Scientists estimate that we've only explored around 5% of the ocean floor, leaving much of its mysteries still waiting to be discovered.

Fact 19: Despite the extreme conditions of the deep sea, life thrives in abundance. From microscopic organisms to giant predators, every inch of this dark and mysterious realm is teeming with activity.

Fact 20: Exploring the deep sea is not for the faint of heart. It requires specialized equipment, years of training, and a healthy dose of curiosity and bravery. But for those who dare to venture into its depths, the rewards are endless, offering glimpses into a world that few have ever seen.

BLOBFISH

Fact 1: Meet the blobfish, a creature so almost cute. This gelatinous fish has a face only a mother could love, with droopy features and a body that looks like a deflated balloon.

Fact 2: But don't let its appearance fool you; the blobfish is perfectly adapted to its deep-sea habitat. Its gelatinous body allows it to float effortlessly in the water, conserving energy in the low-oxygen environment.

Fact 3: In fact, the blobfish's unique anatomy is a prime example of what scientists call "buoyancy adaptation." By having a body that is slightly less dense than the water around it, the

blobfish can stay afloat without
expending much energy.

Fact 4: But here's where it gets really
weird. The blobfish doesn't have a
swim bladder like most fish, which
helps them control their buoyancy.
Instead, its body is made up of a
gelatinous mass that gives it its
distinctive blob-like appearance.

Fact 5: Despite its gelatinous body,
the blobfish is actually a formidable
predator. It feeds on small
invertebrates like crustaceans and
sea urchins, using its fleshy lips to
suck up its prey like a vacuum cleaner.

Fact 6: But life in the deep sea isn't
easy, even for a blobfish. With

pressures reaching up to 120 times that of the surface, the blobfish has to contend with extreme conditions that would crush most other creatures.

Fact 7: To cope with the intense pressure, the blobfish has evolved a body structure that allows it to withstand the weight of the water above it. Its gelatinous flesh acts like a cushion, protecting its internal organs from being crushed.

Fact 8: But perhaps the weirdest thing about the blobfish is its appearance. When it's brought to the surface, it undergoes a dramatic transformation, turning from a gelatinous blob into a saggy, deflated mess.

Fact 9: This is because the blobfish is adapted to the high-pressure environment of the deep sea. When it's brought to the surface, the pressure suddenly decreases, causing its body to lose its shape and collapse in on itself.

Fact 10: Despite its unappealing appearance, the blobfish has become something of an internet sensation in recent years. Its droopy face and comical expression have made it a favorite among meme-makers and internet users.

Fact 11: But while the blobfish may look like a joke, it's actually a crucial part of the deep-sea ecosystem. As a top predator, it helps regulate the population of smaller creatures and maintain the balance of the food chain.

Fact 12: Unfortunately, the blobfish is facing a growing threat from human activities. Overfishing and habitat destruction are putting pressure on its already vulnerable population, raising concerns about its long-term survival.

Fact 13: In fact, the blobfish is listed as "vulnerable" by the International Union for Conservation of Nature (IUCN), meaning it's at risk of

extinction if conservation efforts
aren't stepped up.

Fact 14: But there is hope for the
blobfish yet. Conservation groups and
scientists are working to protect its
deep-sea habitat and raise awareness
about the importance of preserving
this unique and fascinating creature.

Fact 15: Despite its name, the
blobfish isn't actually a blob at all. Its
gelatinous body is made up of a
combination of flesh and fat, giving it
a squishy texture that helps it survive
in the deep sea.

Fact 16: Blobfish are typically found
at depths of around 2,000 to 4,000
feet below the surface, where the

pressure is so intense that few other creatures can survive.

Fact 17: Unlike most fish, which have scales to protect their bodies, the blobfish has a soft, fleshy skin that is easily damaged by predators or rough surfaces.

Fact 18: Despite its lack of scales, the blobfish has a surprisingly robust immune system that helps it fend off infections and diseases in the harsh environment of the deep sea.

Fact 19: Blobfish are solitary creatures, rarely venturing far from their deep-sea homes except during mating season. Even then, they prefer

to stay hidden in the depths, away
from the prying eyes of predators.

Fact 20: But for all its weirdness, the
blobfish is a marvel of evolution,
perfectly adapted to its extreme
habitat. Its gelatinous body, droopy
face, and unassuming demeanor may
make it the butt of jokes, but to
scientists, it's a fascinating example
of the incredible diversity of life on
Earth.

NAKED MOLE RATS

Fact 1: Imagine living in an underground world where the sun never shines, the air is thick with humidity, and the ground is littered with tunnels. Welcome to the bizarre world of naked mole rats, where life is anything but ordinary.

Fact 2: These strange creatures are not your typical rodents. With their hairless bodies, wrinkled skin, and protruding teeth, they look more like a cross between a mole and a wrinkly sausage.

Fact 3: But don't let their appearance fool you; naked mole rats are incredibly resilient animals. They've evolved to thrive in the harsh conditions of their underground habitat, where food and water are scarce and predators lurk around every corner.

Fact 4: One of the most unusual things about naked mole rats is their social structure. Unlike most mammals, which live in family groups or harems, naked mole rats live in large colonies ruled by a single breeding female known as the queen.

Fact 5: The queen is the undisputed leader of the colony, with complete control over the other members. She's the only female allowed to breed, and she'll aggressively defend her position against any challengers.

Fact 6: But here's where it gets really weird. The other members of the colony, known as workers, are sterile and unable to reproduce. Instead, their sole purpose is to serve the queen, gathering food, caring for the young, and maintaining the tunnels.

Fact 7: Despite their lowly status, the workers are fiercely loyal to the queen. They'll even sacrifice themselves to protect her, forming a living shield around her in the event of an attack.

Fact 8: But perhaps the strangest thing about naked mole rats is their longevity. These creatures can live for up to 30 years, making them one of the longest-living rodents on the planet.

Fact 9: Scientists believe that their unusual social structure may hold the key to their longevity. By living in a tightly-knit colony, naked mole rats are able to share resources and protect each other from predators, increasing their chances of survival.

Fact 10: Another factor that may contribute to their longevity is their ability to withstand low oxygen levels. Naked mole rats have a unique respiratory system that allows them to survive in the oxygen-deprived environment of their underground tunnels.

Fact 11: But despite their long lifespan, naked mole rats show few signs of aging. They remain active and healthy well into old age, with no decline in cognitive or physical abilities.

Fact 12: In fact, naked mole rats seem to be immune to many of the diseases that plague other mammals, including cancer. Scientists are studying their unique biology in the hopes of unlocking new treatments for human diseases.

Fact 13: But it's not all sunshine and rainbows for naked mole rats. Their underground lifestyle comes with its own set of challenges, including food shortages, flooding, and attacks from predators like snakes and birds of prey.

Fact 14: To cope with these challenges, naked mole rats have evolved some remarkable adaptations. They can go for long periods without food or water, and they're able to tunnel through soil at an astonishing rate, using their powerful teeth and claws.

Fact 15: But perhaps the most remarkable adaptation of all is their ability to regulate their body temperature. Naked mole rats are able to maintain a constant internal temperature, even in the fluctuating temperatures of their underground habitat.

Fact 16: This ability allows them to survive in environments where other mammals would perish, making them true masters of their underground domain.

Fact 17: Despite their bizarre appearance and unusual lifestyle, naked mole rats are surprisingly cute and cuddly creatures. They're highly social animals, often seen cuddling together in groups to stay warm and cozy.

Fact 18: But don't let their cuddly appearance fool you; naked mole rats are fierce fighters when they need to be. They'll defend their colonies with tooth and claw, driving off intruders and predators with their sheer determination and ferocity.

Fact 19: Despite their small size, naked mole rats play a crucial role in their ecosystem. They help to aerate the soil, control insect populations, and even recycle nutrients by eating plant roots and tubers.

Fact 20: But perhaps their greatest contribution is to science. Naked mole rats have taught us valuable lessons about social behavior, longevity, and disease resistance, offering insights that could one day benefit humans as well.

DUNG BEETLES

Fact 1: Picture this: a beetle rolling a ball of dung across the African savanna. That's the unusual lifestyle of dung beetles, who have a peculiar obsession with poop.

Fact 2: Dung beetles come in all shapes and sizes, from tiny rollers to large tunnelers. But they all share one thing in common: a love for dung.

Fact 3: Why dung, you ask? Well, for dung beetles, poop isn't just waste; it's a valuable resource. They use it to feed themselves, their offspring, and even to build nests.

Fact 4: But it's not just any dung they're after; dung beetles have their preferences. Some species prefer the dung of herbivores, while others go for carnivore or omnivore poop.

Fact 5: Once they've found their preferred poop, dung beetles waste no time getting to work. They'll roll it into a ball, using their hind legs to push and maneuver it across the ground.

Fact 6: But here's where it gets really interesting. Dung beetles use the sun and the stars to navigate, even when they're rolling their dung balls backwards. It's like having a built-in GPS!

Fact 7: And it's not just about transportation; dung beetles also use their dung balls for mating. Males will compete for the largest, most impressive balls, using them to attract females and establish dominance.

Fact 8: But the competition doesn't end there; once a female has chosen a mate, she'll lay her eggs inside the dung ball, providing her offspring with a ready-made source of food.

Fact 9: Some species of dung beetles are even known to bury their dung balls underground, where they'll spend weeks or even months feeding and breeding inside.

Fact 10: But perhaps the weirdest thing about dung beetles is their obsession with dung. They'll go to great lengths to obtain it, even stealing it from other beetles or fighting off competitors for a prized pile of poop.

Fact 11: Despite their lowly reputation, dung beetles play a crucial role in their ecosystems. By burying dung and recycling nutrients, they help to fertilize the soil and promote plant growth.

Fact 12: In fact, some species of dung beetles are so efficient at recycling dung that they're considered valuable allies in agriculture. Farmers have even used them to control pests and reduce the spread of disease.

Fact 13: But it's not just about dung for dung beetles; they'll also feed on other organic matter, including rotting fruit, fungi, and even dead animals.

Fact 14: Dung beetles are found on every continent except Antarctica, where there's not much poop to be found. They've even been spotted at altitudes of over 6,000 meters in the Himalayas, where they feed on the droppings of yaks and other mountain-dwelling animals.

Fact 15: Despite their small size, dung beetles are surprisingly strong. Some species can roll dung balls that are 50 times their own weight, making them one of the strongest animals relative to their size.

Fact 16: But perhaps the most remarkable thing about dung beetles is their diversity. There are over 6,000 species worldwide, each with its own unique adaptations and behaviors.

Fact 17: Some species of dung beetles are even known to exhibit parental care, with mothers staying with their offspring to protect them from predators and provide them with food.

Fact 18: Despite their strange lifestyle, dung beetles are actually quite fascinating creatures. They've evolved a remarkable set of adaptations to thrive in their dung-filled world, from their navigational abilities to their incredible strength.

Fact 19: But perhaps the most important lesson we can learn from dung beetles is the importance of recycling and resourcefulness. These humble creatures may be small, but they play a vital role in keeping ecosystems healthy and functioning.

Fact 20: So the next time you see a dung beetle rolling a ball of poop across the ground, take a moment to appreciate the remarkable ingenuity and resilience of these unsung heroes of the animal kingdom.

AXOLOTLS

Fact 1: Meet the axolotl, a creature straight out of a science fiction novel. These bizarre amphibians look like a cross between a fish and a lizard, with feathery gills sprouting from the sides of their heads.

Fact 2: But what really sets axolotls apart is their remarkable ability to regenerate lost body parts. Unlike most amphibians, which undergo metamorphosis from larval to adult form, axolotls retain their larval features throughout their lives.

Fact 3: This means that if an axolotl loses a limb or even part of its brain, it can regenerate it in a matter of weeks. Scientists are studying this incredible ability in the hopes of unlocking new treatments for human injuries and diseases.

Fact 4: But here's where it gets really weird. Axolotls are one of the few vertebrates capable of regenerating complex structures like limbs, spinal cord, and even parts of their brain.

Fact 5: In fact, axolotls are so good at regenerating that they can even regrow lost organs like their heart, liver, and kidneys. It's like having a built-in repair kit for their bodies!

Fact 6: But despite their remarkable regenerative abilities, axolotls are facing a growing threat from habitat loss and pollution. They're native to the ancient lakes of Mexico, but their numbers have declined dramatically in recent years.

Fact 7: One of the biggest challenges facing axolotls is the loss of their habitat due to urbanization and agriculture. Many of the lakes where they once thrived have been drained or polluted, leaving them with nowhere to go.

Fact 8: Pollution is another major threat to axolotls. Chemicals and pesticides from agricultural runoff can contaminate their water, making it toxic and uninhabitable for these sensitive creatures.

Fact 9: In fact, axolotls are so sensitive to pollution that they're often used as indicator species to assess the health of aquatic ecosystems. If axolotls are thriving, it's a good sign that the ecosystem is healthy and balanced.

Fact 10: But despite the challenges they face, axolotls are surprisingly resilient creatures. They've adapted to survive in the polluted waters of their native lakes, using their regenerative abilities to repair damage caused by toxins.

Fact 11: Another bizarre thing about axolotls is their diet. They're carnivorous creatures, feeding primarily on small fish, insects, and worms. But they'll also eat plant matter and even other axolotls if food is scarce.

Fact 12: Despite their carnivorous nature, axolotls are actually quite docile and gentle creatures. They're popular pets among amphibian enthusiasts, prized for their unique appearance and fascinating behavior.

Fact 13: But perhaps the weirdest thing about axolotls is their ability to breathe through their skin. Like other amphibians, they have lungs for breathing air, but they can also absorb oxygen directly through their skin, allowing them to stay submerged for long periods.

Fact 14: This is especially handy for axolotls, as they're not very good swimmers. Their feathery gills are great for breathing underwater, but they don't provide much propulsion, so they prefer to stay still or walk along the bottom of their habitat.

Fact 15: But despite their awkward swimming style, axolotls are surprisingly agile hunters. They'll lie in wait for unsuspecting prey to swim by, then snap them up with lightning-fast reflexes.

Fact 16: Another weird thing about axolotls is their reproductive habits. Unlike most amphibians, which lay eggs in water, axolotls reproduce by internal fertilization, with the female laying a string of eggs that are fertilized by the male.

Fact 17: But here's where it gets really interesting. Axolotls are capable of both sexual and asexual reproduction, meaning they can reproduce either by mating with a partner or by cloning themselves.

Fact 18: In fact, axolotls are one of the few vertebrates capable of parthenogenesis, a form of asexual reproduction where the female produces offspring without fertilization by a male.

Fact 19: This ability to reproduce asexually has allowed axolotls to colonize new habitats and expand their range, even in the face of habitat loss and pollution.

Fact 20: But despite their remarkable abilities, axolotls are considered critically endangered in the wild. Conservation efforts are underway to protect their remaining habitat and ensure their survival for future generations to marvel at their weird and wonderful ways.

HONEY BADGERS

Fact 1: Meet the honey badger, a small but ferocious creature known for its fearless attitude and tenacious nature. Despite their cute appearance, honey badgers are one of the toughest animals in the world.

Fact 2: Honey badgers are native to Africa and parts of Asia, where they inhabit a wide range of habitats, from savannas and grasslands to forests and deserts.

Fact 3: But what really sets honey badgers apart is their unusual diet. They're omnivores, meaning they'll eat just about anything, from insects and small mammals to fruits, vegetables, and even venomous snakes.

Fact 4: In fact, honey badgers are immune to the venom of many snakes and scorpions, thanks to a specialized protein in their blood that neutralizes toxins.

Fact 5: But perhaps the weirdest thing about honey badgers is their love of honey. They'll go to great lengths to raid beehives, using their sharp claws and powerful jaws to break into the hive and feast on the sweet nectar inside.

Fact 6: But here's where it gets really interesting. Honey badgers are one of the few animals capable of opening a

beehive without getting stung. They'll
cover themselves in mud or dust to
mask their scent, then approach the
hive with stealth and precision.

Fact 7: Once they've raided the hive,
honey badgers will use their long
tongues to lap up the honey,
swallowing it whole before moving on
to the next hive.

Fact 8: But honey badgers aren't just
honey thieves; they're also skilled
hunters. They'll take on prey many
times their size, using their sharp
claws and powerful jaws to subdue
animals much larger and stronger than
themselves.

Fact 9: In fact, honey badgers are known for their tenacity in battle. They'll attack anything that threatens them, from lions and hyenas to humans, using their sharp claws and teeth to inflict serious injury.

Fact 10: But despite their ferocious reputation, honey badgers are actually quite solitary creatures. They prefer to live alone or in small family groups, only coming together to mate or raise young.

Fact 11: Another bizarre thing about honey badgers is their ability to escape from predators by climbing trees. Despite their stocky build and short legs, they're surprisingly agile climbers, using their sharp claws to scramble up trunks and branches with ease.

Fact 12: But perhaps the weirdest thing about honey badgers is their reputation for being indestructible. They've been known to survive attacks from predators like lions and leopards, as well as injuries that would kill most other animals.

Fact 13: In fact, honey badgers are so tough that they've earned the nickname "the most fearless animal in the world." They'll take on anything that comes their way, from venomous snakes to armed humans, without batting an eye.

Fact 14: But despite their tough exterior, honey badgers are actually quite playful creatures. They'll engage in mock fights with each other, rolling around and wrestling like a pair of puppies.

Fact 15: Another bizarre thing about honey badgers is their ability to mimic the sounds of other animals. They'll imitate the calls of birds and mammals to confuse prey or lure them into a trap.

Fact 16: But perhaps the most remarkable thing about honey badgers is their intelligence. They're highly adaptable animals, able to solve complex problems and navigate unfamiliar environments with ease.

Fact 17: In fact, honey badgers have been known to use tools to obtain food, such as using sticks to dig up insects or rocks to break open shells.

Fact 18: But despite their intelligence, honey badgers are facing a growing threat from habitat loss and human encroachment. As their natural habitats are destroyed, they're being forced into closer contact with humans, leading to conflicts and persecution.

Fact 19: In some parts of Africa and Asia, honey badgers are hunted for their fur and meat, or killed by farmers to protect livestock. Conservation efforts are underway to protect their remaining habitat and ensure their survival for future generations.

Fact 20: So the next time you encounter a honey badger, remember to give it the respect it deserves. These small but mighty creatures may be cute and cuddly-looking, but they're also fierce warriors and survivors in the wild.

AYE-AYES

Fact 1: Enter the world of the aye-aye, a creature that looks like a cross between a bat, a raccoon, and a lemur. These bizarre primates are native to Madagascar and are known for their unique appearance and unusual behaviors.

Fact 2: But what really sets aye-ayes apart is their bizarre feeding habits. They're the only primates known to use echolocation to find food, tapping their long, bony fingers on trees to listen for the sounds of grubs and insects hiding inside.

Fact 3: Once they've located their prey, aye-ayes use their sharp incisor teeth to gnaw through the bark of trees, exposing the tasty treats hiding inside.

Fact 4: But here's where it gets really interesting. Aye-ayes have a specialized middle finger that they use to scoop out grubs from their hiding places. It's like having a built-in tool for extracting snacks!

Fact 5: But despite their unique feeding habits, aye-ayes are facing a growing threat from habitat loss and human encroachment. As their forest homes are destroyed, they're being forced into closer contact with humans, leading to conflicts and persecution.

Fact 6: Another bizarre thing about aye-ayes is their appearance. With their large, round eyes, bat-like ears, and long, bushy tails, they look like something out of a nightmare.

Fact 7: But despite their creepy appearance, aye-ayes are actually quite gentle creatures. They're shy and elusive, preferring to stay hidden in the dense foliage of the Madagascar rainforest.

Fact 8: In fact, aye-ayes are so elusive that they were once thought to be extinct. It wasn't until the 1950s that scientists rediscovered them living in the remote forests of Madagascar.

Fact 9: But perhaps the weirdest thing about aye-ayes is their breeding habits. They're solitary animals, only coming together to mate once a year during the breeding season.

Fact 10: But even then, aye-ayes are picky about their partners. Males will engage in elaborate courtship displays to attract females, including vocalizations, scent-marking, and even physical displays like grooming and play-fighting.

Fact 11: Once a female has chosen a mate, she'll give birth to a single offspring after a gestation period of around six months. The baby aye-aye will cling to its mother's belly for the first few months of life, nursing and learning the skills it needs to survive in the forest.

Fact 12: But here's where it gets really interesting. Aye-ayes have a unique way of communicating with each other using a series of clicks and squeaks. These vocalizations help them stay in touch with other members of their species and coordinate their activities in the dense forest.

Fact 13: Despite their solitary nature, aye-ayes are actually quite social animals. They'll form loose alliances with other members of their species, sharing information about food sources and potential threats in their environment.

Fact 14: But perhaps the most remarkable thing about aye-ayes is their intelligence. They're highly adaptable creatures, able to solve complex problems and navigate their environment with ease.

Fact 15: In fact, aye-ayes have been known to use tools to obtain food, such as using sticks to extract insects from tree bark or using leaves as makeshift umbrellas to shelter from the rain.

Fact 16: But despite their intelligence, aye-ayes are facing a growing threat from habitat loss and human encroachment. Conservation efforts are underway to protect their remaining habitat and ensure their survival for future generations.

Fact 17: So the next time you encounter an aye-aye, remember to give it the respect it deserves. These unique and fascinating creatures may look strange, but they're an important part of the Madagascar ecosystem and deserve our protection and admiration.

Fact 18: Aye-ayes are nocturnal creatures, meaning they're most active at night. During the day, they'll sleep in nests made of leaves and branches high up in the trees, away from predators and other threats.

Fact 19: Aye-ayes have a highly developed sense of smell, which they use to locate food and navigate their environment. They have large, sensitive nostrils and a specialized organ in their brain that processes scent information.

Fact 20: Despite their solitary nature, aye-ayes are actually quite vocal animals. They'll use a variety of vocalizations to communicate with each other, including clicks, squeaks, and chirps. These sounds help them stay in touch with other members of their species and coordinate their activities in the dense forest.

BLUE-FOOTED BOOBIES

Fact 1: Let's dive into the fascinating world of the blue-footed booby, a seabird known for its striking blue feet and unique courtship displays. These birds are native to the tropical and subtropical regions of the Pacific Ocean, where they can be found nesting on rocky cliffs and islands.

Fact 2: But what really sets blue-footed boobies apart is their bright blue feet, which are used in elaborate courtship rituals to attract mates. During mating season, males will strut and dance with their feet raised high, showing off their vibrant blue appendages to potential partners.

Fact 3: The bluer the feet, the more attractive the male is to females. It's like having a built-in beauty contest where the winners are determined by the color of their feet!

Fact 4: But here's where it gets really interesting. Blue-footed boobies are known for their sky-pointing behavior, where they'll stand on tiptoe with their beaks pointed upwards and wings outstretched, as if they're posing for a photo shoot.

Fact 5: This behavior is thought to be a form of communication, with males using it to signal their readiness to mate and establish dominance over other males.

Fact 6: But despite their flashy displays, blue-footed boobies are actually quite clumsy on land. They're adapted for life at sea, with webbed feet that make them excellent swimmers but awkward walkers.

Fact 7: In fact, blue-footed boobies spend most of their time at sea, hunting for fish and squid to feed themselves and their chicks. They'll dive from great heights into the water, using their streamlined bodies and sharp beaks to catch their prey.

Fact 8: But despite their prowess as hunters, blue-footed boobies are facing a growing threat from overfishing and habitat loss. As their prey becomes scarce and their nesting sites are destroyed, their populations are declining across their range.

Fact 9: Another bizarre thing about blue-footed boobies is their parenting style. Unlike most birds, which build elaborate nests to protect their eggs and chicks, blue-footed boobies lay their eggs directly on the ground, often in shallow depressions or on rocky ledges.

Fact 10: But here's where it gets really interesting. Blue-footed boobies have a unique way of incubating their eggs, using their webbed feet to tuck them under their bodies and keep them warm. It's like having a built-in incubator!

Fact 11: Once the chicks hatch, both parents take turns feeding and caring for them until they're old enough to fend for themselves. It's a team effort that ensures the survival of the next generation of blue-footed boobies.

Fact 12: Despite their awkward appearance on land, blue-footed boobies are graceful flyers. They have long, pointed wings that allow them to soar effortlessly on the ocean breeze, covering vast distances in search of food.

Fact 13: In fact, blue-footed boobies are known for their long-distance migrations, with some individuals traveling thousands of kilometers between their breeding and feeding grounds each year.

Fact 14: But perhaps the weirdest thing about blue-footed boobies is their mating habits. During mating season, males will perform elaborate courtship displays to attract females, including dancing, sky-pointing, and showing off their vibrant blue feet.

Fact 15: Females will choose their mates based on the quality of their displays, with the bluest-footed males being the most desirable. It's like a colorful dance-off where the winners get the girl!

Fact 16: But despite their flashy courtship displays, blue-footed

boobies are actually quite
monogamous. Once a pair has bonded,
they'll stay together for life, raising
multiple broods of chicks together
over the years.

Fact 17: Another bizarre thing about
blue-footed boobies is their diet.
They're piscivores, meaning they
primarily eat fish, but they'll also
feed on squid, crustaceans, and other
marine creatures.

Fact 18: But here's where it gets
really interesting. Blue-footed
boobies are expert divers, capable of
plunging into the water from great
heights to catch their prey. They'll
fold their wings back and tuck their
feet in close to their bodies,

streamlining themselves for a swift and efficient dive.

Fact 19: Despite their skill as hunters, blue-footed boobies face stiff competition for food from other seabirds, including gulls, pelicans, and frigatebirds. They'll often have to compete with these birds for the same fish, leading to intense feeding frenzies and aerial battles over the open ocean.

Fact 20: Despite the challenges they face, blue-footed boobies are resilient birds, able to adapt to changing conditions and thrive in their oceanic habitat. They're a symbol of the beauty and diversity of the natural world, reminding us of the

importance of protecting our oceans
and the creatures that call them
home.

PANGOLINS

Fact 1: Welcome to the world of pangolins, the only mammals covered in scales. These unique creatures are native to Africa and Asia, where they inhabit a variety of habitats, from forests and grasslands to savannas and deserts.

Fact 2: But what really sets pangolins apart is their incredible armor-like scales, which cover their entire bodies and provide protection from predators. When threatened, pangolins will curl up into a tight ball, using their scales as a shield against attackers.

Fact 3: But here's where it gets really interesting. Pangolins are the only mammals known to have true scales made of keratin, the same protein found in human hair and nails. These scales are incredibly tough and durable, making pangolins virtually impervious to most predators.

Fact 4: In fact, pangolins are so well-armored that even lions, hyenas, and leopards have trouble breaking through their defenses. Their only real threat is humans, who hunt them for their scales, which are believed to have medicinal properties in some cultures.

Fact 5: But despite their formidable defenses, pangolins are facing a growing threat from habitat loss and poaching. As their forest homes are cleared for agriculture and urban development, their populations are declining across their range.

Fact 6: Another bizarre thing about pangolins is their diet. They're insectivores, meaning they primarily eat ants and termites, which they catch with their long, sticky tongues.

Fact 7: But here's where it gets really interesting. Pangolins have incredibly long tongues, which can reach lengths of up to 16 inches. They use these tongues to probe deep into ant and termite nests, lapping up insects with lightning-fast reflexes.

Fact 8: But despite their voracious appetite for insects, pangolins are actually quite picky eaters. They'll only eat certain species of ants and termites, preferring those with soft bodies and high nutritional value.

Fact 9: In fact, pangolins have been known to consume up to 70 million insects in a single year, making them one of the most efficient pest controllers in the animal kingdom.

Fact 10: But perhaps the weirdest thing about pangolins is their reproductive habits. They're solitary animals, only coming together to mate once a year during the breeding season.

Fact 11: Males will engage in elaborate courtship displays to attract females, including vocalizations, scent-marking, and even physical displays like grooming and play-fighting.

Fact 12: Once a female has chosen a mate, she'll give birth to a single offspring after a gestation period of around five months. The baby pangolin, known as a pup, will cling to its mother's belly for the first few months of life, nursing and learning the skills it needs to survive in the wild.

Fact 13: Another bizarre thing about pangolins is their ability to defend themselves. When threatened, they'll curl up into a tight ball, using their tough scales as armor against predators.

Fact 14: But here's where it gets really interesting. Pangolins can also release a noxious-smelling fluid from glands near their anus, which they use to deter attackers. It's like having a built-in stink bomb!

Fact 15: Despite their unique adaptations for defense, pangolins are still vulnerable to poaching and habitat loss. Conservation efforts are underway to protect their remaining habitat and ensure their survival for future generations.

Fact 16: Pangolins are often called "scaly anteaters" because of their diet and appearance. Like anteaters, they have long, sticky tongues for catching insects, but unlike anteaters, they're covered in tough, overlapping scales.

Fact 17: Pangolins are excellent climbers and can often be found high up in the trees, where they hunt for insects and seek shelter from predators.

Fact 18: Despite their tough exterior, pangolins are actually quite gentle creatures. They're shy and elusive, preferring to stay hidden in the dense foliage of their forest homes.

Fact 19: Pangolins are highly adapted for life on the ground, with powerful claws for digging and burrowing. They'll often excavate underground tunnels and burrows to escape from predators and harsh weather conditions.

Fact 20: Pangolins play a crucial role in their ecosystems as insectivores and seed dispersers. By controlling insect populations and spreading seeds, they help to maintain the balance of their forest habitats and promote plant growth.

YETI CRABS

Fact 1: Deep beneath the ocean's surface, in the dark and frigid depths of the deep sea, lives a creature straight out of a horror movie: the yeti crab. These bizarre crustaceans are found in the cold waters of the Pacific Ocean, where they inhabit hydrothermal vents and cold seeps.

Fact 2: But what really sets yeti crabs apart is their bizarre appearance. Covered in long, silky white hairs, they look like miniature yetis, the legendary abominable snowmen of the Himalayas.

Fact 3: These hairs are not just for show; they're actually a form of camouflage, helping yeti crabs blend in with their surroundings and avoid detection by predators.

Fact 4: But here's where it gets really interesting. Yeti crabs are not just passive inhabitants of the deep sea; they're actually active hunters, using their specialized claws to catch small prey like shrimp and plankton.

Fact 5: Their claws are covered in fine hairs, which they use to filter particles from the water and trap tiny organisms for food. It's like having built-in fishing nets attached to their arms!

Fact 6: But despite their fearsome appearance, yeti crabs are actually quite docile creatures. They're not aggressive towards each other and will often congregate in large groups around hydrothermal vents, where they feed on the rich nutrients carried by the water.

Fact 7: In fact, yeti crabs are so well adapted to life in the deep sea that they have evolved specialized bacteria in their gills, which help them to extract energy from the toxic chemicals found in hydrothermal vents.

Fact 8: Another bizarre thing about yeti crabs is their reproductive habits. They're ovoviviparous, meaning that they give birth to live young rather than laying eggs like most other crustaceans.

Fact 9: Females will carry their eggs in a brood pouch on their abdomen until they hatch, protecting them from predators and providing them with nutrients until they're ready to fend for themselves.

Fact 10: But here's where it gets really interesting. Yeti crabs are known for their unique method of parental care. After the eggs hatch, the mother will release a cloud of tiny larvae into the water, where they'll drift and feed on plankton until they're large enough to settle on the seafloor.

Fact 11: Yeti crabs are found in some of the most extreme environments on Earth, including hydrothermal vents and cold seeps, where they endure high pressures, freezing temperatures, and toxic chemicals.

Fact 12: But despite these harsh conditions, yeti crabs are thriving in their deep-sea habitats, thanks to their specialized adaptations and unique reproductive strategies.

Fact 13: Yeti crabs are not just fascinating creatures in their own right; they're also important indicators of the health of deep-sea ecosystems. By studying their behavior and abundance, scientists can learn valuable insights into the complex dynamics of life in the deep sea.

Fact 14: Despite their fearsome appearance, yeti crabs are actually quite small, with adults reaching lengths of just a few centimeters. They're well adapted to their environment, with flattened bodies and long, delicate limbs that allow them to maneuver through the rocky terrain of the deep sea.

Fact 15: Yeti crabs are highly specialized feeders, with their hairy claws adapted for capturing small organisms from the water. They'll use their claws to scrape algae and bacteria from the surfaces of rocks and other substrates, as well as to catch drifting particles of organic matter.

Fact 16: Another bizarre thing about yeti crabs is their symbiotic relationship with chemosynthetic bacteria. These bacteria live in the hairs covering the crabs' bodies and gills, where they convert toxic chemicals from hydrothermal vents into energy through a process known as chemosynthesis.

Fact 17: In return for providing them with energy, the bacteria receive shelter and a constant supply of nutrients from the crab's body. It's a mutually beneficial arrangement that allows both species to thrive in the harsh conditions of the deep sea.

Fact 18: Yeti crabs are often found in dense clusters around hydrothermal vents and cold seeps, where they feed on the rich nutrients carried by the water. These clusters can consist of hundreds or even thousands of individuals, creating a bustling community in the depths of the ocean.

Fact 19: Despite their bizarre appearance and extreme habitat, yeti crabs are surprisingly fragile creatures. They're sensitive to changes in temperature, water chemistry, and other environmental factors, making them vulnerable to disturbances from human activities such as deep-sea mining and oil drilling.

Fact 20: Conservation efforts are underway to protect yeti crabs and their deep-sea habitats from these threats, ensuring that these unique and fascinating creatures will continue to thrive in the dark and mysterious depths of the ocean for generations to come.

STAR-NOSED MOLES

Fact 1: Enter the world of the star-nosed mole, a creature with a truly bizarre and fascinating adaptation: a star-shaped appendage on its nose. These small mammals are found in the wetlands and marshes of eastern North America, where they spend their days burrowing through the soil in search of food.

Fact 2: But what really sets star-nosed moles apart is their remarkable sense of touch. The star-shaped appendage on their nose is covered in over 22,000 tiny sensory receptors, called Eimer's organs, which allow them to detect prey with incredible precision.

Fact 3: These sensory receptors are so sensitive that star-nosed moles can detect minute vibrations in the soil caused by the movements of their prey, such as earthworms, insects, and small crustaceans.

Fact 4: But here's where it gets really interesting. Star-nosed moles are one of the fastest foraging mammals in the world, capable of detecting and consuming prey in as little as 230 milliseconds – faster than the blink of an eye!

Fact 5: In fact, star-nosed moles are so efficient at finding food that they can consume up to half their body weight in prey every day, making them one of the most voracious predators in their ecosystem.

Fact 6: Another bizarre thing about star-nosed moles is their unique method of hunting. Unlike most moles, which rely primarily on their sense of smell to locate prey, star-nosed moles use their specialized nose to feel their way through the dark underground tunnels where they live.

Fact 7: But despite their remarkable adaptations for hunting, star-nosed moles are not immune to predation themselves. They're often targeted by predators such as owls, hawks, foxes, and snakes, which use their keen senses to locate the moles' burrows and ambush them while they're above ground.

Fact 8: Yet despite these threats, star-nosed moles are highly successful animals, thanks to their unique adaptations and behaviors. They're able to thrive in a variety of habitats, from dense forests to open meadows, and play a crucial role in their ecosystems as predators and soil engineers.

Fact 9: Star-nosed moles are solitary creatures, spending most of their lives alone except during the breeding season. Males will establish territories and defend them from intruders, while females will raise their young in underground burrows lined with grass and leaves.

Fact 10: But here's where it gets really interesting. Star-nosed moles are one of the few mammals that are known to be monogamous, forming long-term pair bonds with their mates and raising multiple litters of pups together over the course of their lives.

Fact 11: Another bizarre thing about star-nosed moles is their reproductive habits. Females give birth to litters of three to seven pups in the spring, after a gestation period of about 45 days. The pups are born blind and hairless, but they quickly develop and are weaned after just a few weeks.

Fact 12: But despite their remarkable adaptations for underground life, star-nosed moles are not completely blind. They have small eyes with reduced vision, which they use to detect light and movement in their dark subterranean environment.

Fact 13: In addition to their unique sense of touch, star-nosed moles also have an excellent sense of smell, which they use to locate mates, detect predators, and navigate their underground tunnels.

Fact 14: But perhaps the weirdest thing about star-nosed moles is their appearance. With their small, stocky bodies and distinctive star-shaped noses, they look like creatures straight out of a science fiction movie.

Fact 15: Despite their unusual appearance, star-nosed moles are fascinating creatures with a range of unique adaptations and behaviors. They're an important part of their ecosystems, helping to control insect populations and aerate the soil with their burrowing activities.

Fact 16: Star-nosed moles are highly territorial animals, using scent markings and vocalizations to establish and defend their territories from intruders. They'll often engage in aggressive encounters with rival males, using their powerful claws and sharp teeth to assert dominance and protect their turf.

Fact 17: Despite their solitary nature, star-nosed moles are not entirely antisocial. They'll sometimes engage in cooperative behaviors, such as sharing food or grooming each other, especially during the breeding season when males and females come together to mate and raise their young.

Fact 18: Star-nosed moles are excellent diggers, using their powerful forelimbs and sharp claws to excavate complex underground burrows. These burrows can extend for several meters underground and contain multiple chambers for sleeping, nesting, and storing food.

Fact 19: Despite their underground lifestyle, star-nosed moles are excellent swimmers and will often forage for food in marshes, ponds, and streams. They'll use their webbed feet and paddle-like tails to propel themselves through the water and catch aquatic prey such as fish, tadpoles, and aquatic insects.

Fact 20: Conservation efforts are underway to protect star-nosed moles and their wetland habitats from threats such as habitat loss, pollution, and climate change. By preserving these unique and fascinating creatures, we can ensure that future

generations will continue to marvel at
their strange and wonderful
adaptations.

PINK FAIRY ARMADILLOS

Fact 1: Welcome to the world of the pink fairy armadillo, one of the smallest and least-known species of armadillo. These tiny creatures are native to the deserts and scrublands of central Argentina, where they spend their days burrowing underground and avoiding the scorching heat of the sun.

Fact 2: But what really sets pink fairy armadillos apart is their unique appearance. They're covered in a thin, flexible shell made of keratin, the same material found in human fingernails and hair, which protects them from predators and helps them retain moisture in their arid environment.

Fact 3: Despite their name, pink fairy armadillos are not actually pink. They have pale pinkish-brown fur covering their bodies, which helps them blend in with the sandy soils of their desert habitat.

Fact 4: But here's where it gets really interesting. Pink fairy armadillos have an incredibly flattened shell, which allows them to squeeze into tight spaces and burrow through the loose sand with ease. They're like tiny, armored submarines navigating the underground tunnels of their desert home!

Fact 5: In addition to their flattened shell, pink fairy armadillos also have powerful claws on their forelimbs, which they use to dig and excavate their burrows. These claws are adapted for digging in sandy soils, allowing the armadillos to create complex networks of tunnels and chambers beneath the surface.

Fact 6: Despite their adaptations for digging, pink fairy armadillos are not particularly fast or agile on land. They're slow-moving creatures, preferring to conserve energy by burrowing underground during the hottest parts of the day and emerging at night to forage for food.

Fact 7: Another bizarre thing about pink fairy armadillos is their diet. They're insectivores, meaning they primarily eat insects and other invertebrates found in the soil, such as ants, termites, and beetle larvae.

Fact 8: But here's where it gets really interesting. Pink fairy armadillos have a specialized tongue covered in sticky saliva, which they use to capture and consume their prey. It's like having a built-in insect trap attached to their mouths!

Fact 9: Despite their small size, pink fairy armadillos are surprisingly long-lived, with lifespans of up to 15 years in captivity. In the wild, they face threats from predators such as foxes, owls, and snakes, as well as habitat loss and fragmentation due to human activities.

Fact 10: Pink fairy armadillos are solitary creatures, spending most of their lives alone except during the breeding season. Males will establish territories and defend them from intruders, while females will raise their young in underground burrows lined with grass and leaves.

Fact 11: But despite their solitary nature, pink fairy armadillos are not entirely antisocial. They'll sometimes share their burrows with other individuals, especially during the breeding season when males and

females come together to mate and
raise their young.

Fact 12: Pink fairy armadillos are
excellent diggers, using their powerful
forelimbs and sharp claws to excavate
complex underground burrows. These
burrows can extend for several
meters underground and contain
multiple chambers for sleeping,
nesting, and storing food.

Fact 13: In addition to their
burrowing activities, pink fairy
armadillos also play a crucial role in
their desert ecosystems as soil
engineers. By digging and aerating the
soil, they help to improve its
structure and fertility, making it more

suitable for plant growth and supporting a diverse range of wildlife.

Fact 14: Despite their adaptations for life in the desert, pink fairy armadillos are sensitive to changes in their environment. They're vulnerable to disturbances from human activities such as habitat destruction, pollution, and climate change, which threaten their survival and the health of their ecosystems.

Fact 15: Conservation efforts are underway to protect pink fairy armadillos and their desert habitats from these threats. By preserving their unique and fascinating species, we can ensure that future generations

will continue to marvel at their
strange and wonderful adaptations.

SAIGA ANTELOPES

Fact 1: Let's explore the unique world of the saiga antelope, a creature with a distinctive appearance and a fascinating history. These peculiar animals are native to the grasslands and semi-arid steppes of central Asia, where they roam in small herds in search of food and water.

Fact 2: But what really sets saiga antelopes apart is their unusual nose. They have long, tubular noses that hang down over their mouths, giving them a somewhat comical appearance. But this nose serves a crucial purpose: it helps filter out dust and warm up cold air during the harsh winters on the steppes.

Fact 3: In addition to their unique noses, saiga antelopes are also known for their distinctive horns. Both males and females have horns, which are curved and pointed, with ridges along their length. These horns are used for defense against predators and for establishing dominance within their herds.

Fact 4: But here's where it gets really interesting. Saiga antelopes are highly adapted to life on the open plains, with long legs and a streamlined body that allows them to run at high speeds to escape from predators such as wolves and snow leopards.

Fact 5: Despite their adaptations for speed and agility, saiga antelopes are facing a growing threat from habitat loss and hunting. As their grassland habitats are converted to agricultural land and their populations are targeted by poachers for their horns, their numbers have declined dramatically in recent years.

Fact 6: Another bizarre thing about saiga antelopes is their breeding habits. They're seasonal breeders, coming together in large herds during the mating season to mate and give birth to their young.

Fact 7: Males will compete for the attention of females, engaging in elaborate displays of strength and dominance to attract mates. They'll lock horns and push and shove each other in fierce battles for dominance within the herd.

Fact 8: Once a female has chosen a mate, she'll give birth to a single calf after a gestation period of around five months. The calf will stay close to its mother for the first few weeks of life, nursing and learning the skills it needs to survive in the harsh environment of the steppes.

Fact 9: But here's where it gets really interesting. Saiga antelopes are known for their incredible migratory behavior, undertaking epic journeys across vast distances in search of food and water.

Fact 10: During the winter months, when the steppes are covered in snow and ice, saiga antelopes will migrate south to warmer, more hospitable climates, where they can find grasses and shrubs to feed on. Then, when the weather warms up in the spring, they'll migrate back north to their breeding grounds to mate and give birth.

Fact 11: Despite their incredible adaptability and resilience, saiga antelopes are facing a growing threat from climate change. As temperatures rise and weather patterns become more unpredictable, their traditional migratory routes are becoming

disrupted, making it harder for them
to find food and water.

Fact 12: In addition to climate change,
saiga antelopes are also vulnerable to
disease outbreaks, which can
decimate their populations in a matter
of weeks. In recent years, outbreaks
of disease such as pasteurellosis and
hemorrhagic septicemia have killed
thousands of saiga antelopes, posing a
serious threat to their survival.

Fact 13: Conservation efforts are
underway to protect saiga antelopes
and their grassland habitats from
these threats. By establishing
protected areas, implementing anti-
poaching measures, and raising
awareness about the importance of

preserving these unique and fascinating creatures, we can ensure that saiga antelopes will continue to roam the steppes for generations to come.

Fact 14: Despite their somewhat comical appearance, saiga antelopes are highly adapted to their harsh environment, with thick fur coats that help them stay warm during the bitter winters and long legs that allow them to run at high speeds to escape from predators.

Fact 15: Saiga antelopes are highly social animals, forming large herds of up to several hundred individuals during the mating season. These herds provide safety in numbers, allowing the antelopes to defend themselves against predators and share information about food and water sources.

Fact 16: Another bizarre thing about saiga antelopes is their diet. They're herbivores, feeding primarily on grasses, shrubs, and other vegetation found on the steppes. They'll use their long, pointed noses to graze on the tough, dry grasses that grow in the arid landscape.

Fact 17: But despite their adaptations for life on the open plains, saiga antelopes are not immune to predation. They're often targeted by wolves, snow leopards, and other predators, which use their keen senses and stealthy hunting tactics to ambush the antelopes while they're grazing or resting.

Fact 18: Saiga antelopes play a crucial role in their grassland ecosystems as grazers and seed dispersers. By feeding on grasses and other vegetation, they help to maintain the balance of plant populations and promote the growth of new vegetation through their droppings.

Fact 19: Despite their importance to the ecosystem, saiga antelopes are facing a growing threat from human activities such as habitat destruction, hunting, and climate change. Conservation efforts are underway to protect their remaining habitats and ensure their survival for future generations.

Fact 20: By preserving these unique and fascinating creatures and the grasslands they call home, we can ensure that saiga antelopes will continue to roam the steppes for generations to come, providing beauty and wonder to all who encounter them.

www.ingramcontent.com/pod-product-compliance
Lightning Source LLC
Chambersburg PA
CBHW061055250726
48653CB00001B/415